How To Help Someone With Anxiety

The Ultimate Guide on How To Help a Friend With Anxiety

Edward Katherine

Table of Contents

Chapter 1

Understanding Anxiety

We've all experienced anxiety and are familiar with the sensations that come with it, such as feeling tense and edgy, having a butterfly feeling in our stomach, our heart racing, being out of breath, feeling hot and sticky, and having difficulty focusing or concentrating.

Although unpleasant, anxiety has served us well as an emotion throughout our evolutionary history. Without it, we would not have been able to adjust our behaviors as easily to the hazards we faced. When attachment conduct is prompted in part by anxiety, children will not seek the safety of their parents. We wouldn't be as conscious of risks to our position in the tribe's social structures, which is critical for survival. We would not be able to detect risks in the world as quickly, and our bodies would not immediately prepare to 'fight' or 'flight' in times of peril. Even the most painful sensations, such as increased breathing rates, beating hearts, and sweating, are our bodies natural response to threats and help us prepare for active activity to confront or avoid the dangers we face.

Unfortunately, this fear, as well as the neurological hard wiring that underpins it, can cause some of us to experience excessive, severe, and chronic anxiety, which begins to rule and control our lives. Some of us may feel continually threatened and frightened, which we refer to as generalized anxiety. Others may have quick and acute anxiety, even panic, induced by specific items such as a spider phobia, an intense dread of heights, or simply being outside.

Others have significant dread of being evaluated socially, which is known as social anxiety or anxiety tied to triggers associated with specific traumas, such as a loud noise triggering flashbacks in a soldier suffering from PTSD. Excessive troublesome anxiety is one of the most frequent mental health issues we face, with 37.1% of women and 29.9% of men experiencing high levels of anxiety in 2022.

Anxiety disorders can be classified into several major types:

Panic disorder is characterized by recurring panic attacks accompanied by symptoms such as sweating, trembling, shortness of breath, or a sense of choking; a pounding heart or high heart rate; and emotions of fear. These kinds of attacks usually happen suddenly and without warning. People who have panic attacks frequently become concerned about when the next episode may occur, which can cause them to alter or limit their typical activities.

Phobias are severe dread of certain objects, such as spiders or snakes, or circumstances, such as flying in planes that are distressing or invasive.

Generalized anxiety disorder is defined by chronic worry or anxiety. People suffering from this disease are concerned about a variety of issues, including health problems and finances, and they may have a general sense that something horrible will happen. Symptoms include nervousness, agitation muscle tension, difficulty concentrating, sleep disturbances, and a general sense of unease.

Social anxiety disorder is also called social phobia. People with this illness are afraid of social situations where they can be embarrassed or judged. They are often uneasy when socializing, self-conscious in front of others, and concerned about being rejected or offending others. Other common symptoms include difficulty establishing friends, avoiding social situations, fretting for days before a social function, and feeling shaky, hot, or queasy while in a social environment.

Obsessive-compulsive disorder is distinguished by persistent, uncontrollable thoughts and emotions (obsessions) and repetitive or ritualistic behaviors (compulsions). Some common instances include obsessive hand washing due to a fear of germs or constantly scrutinizing work for faults.

Posttraumatic stress disorder (PTSD) can occur in response to a severe physical or emotional trauma, such as a natural disaster, tragic accident, or crime. Symptoms include flashbacks to the trauma, nightmares, and disturbing thoughts that disrupt a person's daily routine for months or years following the traumatic incident.

Once this is recognized and patients begin to normalize their experiences, we may begin to investigate why their anxiety has become so severe in their specific circumstances. For example, some people appear to be born with a higher anxiety threshold, whilst others are influenced by their formative experiences. Others may relate their anxiety to an early time of severe stress. In almost every case, people's attempts to avoid situations that make them uneasy exacerbate and entrench the primary source of their worry. For example, someone who suffers from agoraphobia maintains their anxiety by believing that they are only safe because they have not gone outside. Their avoidance reinforces their anxiety because they do not have the opportunity to learn that stepping outside is actually safe!

Developing a thorough knowledge of the reasons of a person's anxiety is an important first step in establishing a treatment plan together. This differs depending on the type of anxiety and the underlying causes, but all therapy options focus on assisting people in identifying and changing how they understand and manage their anxiety.

This includes assisting someone in identifying and challenging the unhelpful ideas that can fuel and perpetuate their anxiety. It nearly always entails assisting someone to 'front their fear' in a gradual manner, so that they finally learn through experience that they no longer need to be so nervous and that the outcomes they dreaded, which underlying their worry, will not occur.

Using ways to help people relax, reduce stress, and stay grounded is also beneficial. Sometimes it is necessary to assist people in correctly processing the underlying causes of their anxiety so that past events do not interfere with people's capacity to live effectively in the present.

Chapter 2

Recognize Anxiety in Others

If you suspect a friend, coworker, or loved one has an anxiety problem and want to help them, the first step is to talk to them about it, because you can't help your friend unless they agree to accept your support. But how do you know if they're dealing with anxiety in the first place, especially if your friend or loved one isn't sure? Anxiety disorders, like many other mood disorders, can be difficult to detect since, unlike obvious diseases, patients do not walk around with red spots and fever. If you know what you're searching for, it's easy to tell whether he or she is simply overly sensitive or suffering from something more serious and disturbing.

Anxiety disorder is a broad term that encompasses numerous types of anxiety disorders acknowledged by the professional psychological community. While you cannot diagnose your buddy with a specific anxiety illness or anxiety disorder in general, you may inform them that you have seen that they appear to be struggling recently and encourage them to seek help.

Here are some signals that a friend or family member may have an anxiety problem; if you bring these symptoms up, be tactful, and patient, and let them know that you care about and support them above all else.

Their Body Language
One of the most common indications of anxiety is persistent muscle tightness. People with anxiety disorders frequently complain of aching limbs and jaws as a result of continual clenching, even if they are unaware of it. According to the Anxiety Centre, this tension can affect all parts of the body, so if you notice your friend clenching their fists, tapping their feet, or generally being unable to keep still while clearly in a state of high mental and physical agitation on multiple occasions, consider it a sign of possible anxiety problems.

Chest Pains or Racing Heart

In some specific symptoms of anxiety, such as panic attacks, the body rushes into adrenaline excess, flooding with hormones to stimulate a "fight or flight" reaction. The fight or flight reaction, also known as the "acute stress response," puts the body on high alert, ready to meet threats to its survival or run blindly to preserve itself, even if the circumstance is not life-threatening. One part of this response is a hammering heart rate as the body seeks to provide as much oxygen to its limbs as possible.

If your buddy complains of having their pulse race unexpectedly, especially when they are anxious or stressed, it may be an indication that they need professional help.

The Feeling of Being On Edge

This is especially essential for persons suffering from generalized anxiety disorder. People suffering from generalized anxiety disorder are constantly on the lookout for risks and frightened responses to emergencies. Your acquaintance may not tell you directly, but they will most likely give out subconscious and cognitive signals that they are ready to jump at any time. Pacing, speaking too quickly, reacting forcefully to external noises or stimuli, or being highly restless are all signs that they are ready to act, even if there is nothing to react to.

They Express Fears That Appear Catastrophic

A mind that isn't caught up in the same cycle of ideas that cause worry can find it entirely baffling. Obsessive-compulsive disorder is perhaps the most well-known manifestation of this drive, and it can be perplexing to people who do not suffer from it. The compulsive acts that those who suffer from this disorder are driven to engage in, from closing a door multiple times to washing hands, are aimed at dealing with the discomfort caused by the obsessive thoughts and relieving the nervousness they are feeling.

However, stressful, catastrophizing thoughts are not exclusive to OCD; they are also common in other anxiety disorders. Anxious persons may dwell on the worst possible conclusion of a situation, no matter how unlikely it is, and obsess over it, unable to convince themselves of its relative impossibility. This is known as "catastrophizing," and it can be paralyzing. Anxiety stems from a deep place and is frequently impossible to talk or dismiss rationally.

They Sleep Poorly
According to the Psychiatric Times, anxiety disorders and insomnia are frequently associated: insomnia is one of the criteria used to officially diagnose someone with an anxiety disorder, based on the Diagnostic Statistical Manual (DSM), a resource for mental health professionals. The reasoning is actually quite simple: if your friend is pumped up, alert, and on the lookout for threats, or unable to stop the catastrophizing ideas racing through their mind, they are unlikely to be able to relax and sleep well.

They're Irritable
We all get snappy from time to time, and there are numerous reasons why a person may be persistently irritable, as well as the fact that not all persons with anxiety problems are irritable. However, because persons with untreated anxiety disorders frequently experience poor sleep, tension, and repeated adrenaline surges, irritability is common.

There are also other reasons why an anxious person may be easily upset. Those who suffer from anxiety attacks may be more irritable due to their inability to cope with worrisome thoughts; this type of hyper-vigilance may result in a short fuse when dealing with persons in their space or occupying their attention.

They need things done in a certain way to maintain a sense of control.
Though we may think of this behavior as primarily a component of the compulsive elements of obsessive-compulsive disorder, behavior designed to deal with or somehow "confront" a catastrophic event that an anxious person believes is likely to happen, it can also be part of the rest of the anxiety spectrum. One way you can cope with anxiety is to overcompensate by exercising complete control over your current surroundings, including the people around you. Your worried buddy may want to maintain control and micromanage, not

because they are dictatorial, but because they believe it is necessary to avoid disaster.

They avoid situations that cause too much worry

The precise name for avoiding something, because it has the potential to induce anxiety, is "avoidance coping," and it is the most essential aspect of anxiety. This inclination is an extension of the anxious person's attempt to hyper-manage their environment, except that the control manifests as avoiding any circumstance deemed to be a potential powder keg. This tendency may be difficult to detect in friends; it is easier if their specific anxiety is a social anxiety disorder, in which case their avoidance will be focused on social events. However, if it's other things that make them compulsively worried, or just life in general, you may have to look harder to determine what they're excluding from their lives: certain circumstances, people, hobbies, or things that they believe cause major worry and avoid.

They Cannot Be "Talked Down" Easily

If someone who does not have an anxiety illness is concerned, you may typically address their concerns and explore their feelings logically. People with anxiety disorders do not have the kinds of anxieties that respond to this type of treatment; there's very nothing you, as a friend, can do to bring them "out" of a spiral of worried thinking or panic attacks. This is because anxiety-related concerns are not reasonable, and thus cannot be rationalized. Serious anxiety treatment requires therapy, which may leave you feeling useless or unable to help as a friend or family member, but you can help in a variety of ways, from physically supporting your friend during bad episodes to assisting them in challenging certain aspects of their fears on their own.

Chapter 3

Communicating With Someone Who is Anxious

People with anxiety disorders overthink and are more sensitive to words or triggers, which can make communication difficult. Our words have power, and people who suffer from severe anxiety frequently internalize them more thoroughly. People who are anxious may be more sensitive to what others say.

Anxiety is, nevertheless, prevalent; figures show that about one-third of teenagers suffer from an anxiety disorder, and roughly the same number of adults have been diagnosed with one at some point in their lives. This suggests that someone in your life is most certainly experiencing anxiety, and you will need to learn how to communicate with them.

The good news is that you can have a productive conversation with someone who is worried if you have a little knowledge, patience, curiosity, and compassion. We'll go over therapist-approved suggestions for things to say and not say to someone who is experiencing anxiety below, along with practical actions you may take to help them. The following are things you should not say to someone who has an anxiety problem.

Calm down

Although it may appear rational to you, urging someone with anxiety to relax is not an effective method. At best, it may appear invalidating or condescending; at worst, it may cause a panic attack. Using this language suggests that an anxious person's sentiments are invalid. This can make them feel as if you're not taking their anxiety seriously or don't understand what they're going through, which can exacerbate nervous feelings.

Furthermore, merely telling someone with anxiety to calm down indicates an insufficient grasp of anxiety; it is like telling someone with a broken arm to walk it off. Anxiety is not something you can easily turn off. An anxious individual cannot just cease being nervous. It does not operate like that. In truth, anxiety is a mental health issue that frequently necessitates expert help.

Try not to discount your loved one's pain, even if you don't comprehend what they're going through or believe their fears are illogical. Remember that urging someone to relax does not help their anxiety go away. Instead, try to identify with what they're going through.

You should have more confidence
This is something I frequently hear from clients who are experiencing workplace anxiety. The difficulty is that persons with anxiety suffer from self-doubt. Anxiety is frequently accompanied by self-doubt.

Supervisors and others who use this type of rhetoric may believe they are empowering. Telling someone with anxiety to be confident does not address the underlying reasons that are undermining their confidence, such as a lack of experience, impostor syndrome, or fear of failure.

This type of advice can be detrimental, as it may make the person believe that their lack of confidence is a personal flaw rather than a normal part of the learning process. Instead, collaborate with a nervous individual to find strategies to boost their confidence.

Stop being pessimistic" or "be positive
Anxious people are more prone to negative thinking and rumination, which can be a difficult habit to break. When we are anxious, we are more likely to listen to the negative voice. However, simply being positive is not enough to overcome this negative voice. Anxiety cannot be turned on or off.

Positive affirmations have been demonstrated to reduce anxiety, enhance self-esteem, and make people feel less threatened, but only if the individual uttering them understands the message. So, if someone is open to it, this could be a worthwhile method to attempt.

Just breathe

Breathing is an extremely effective method for anxiety relief. But it's not a one-size-fits-all strategy, so it might not be appropriate for everyone. Instead, ask someone with anxiety whether they have a favorite coping method. This could involve breathing exercises, mindfulness practices, or other anxiety-management strategies. Some advised strategies include boxed breathing and the 5-4-3-2-1 mindfulness practice.

There is nothing to stress about

A widespread misperception regarding anxiety is that it only occurs when someone is exposed to stressors. While some conditions, such as social situations or life transitions, might cause a person to acquire anxiety, anxiety can also occur when a person's life is full of so-called positive experiences.

In actuality, there are other causes of anxiety other than life events, including genetics, environment, and neurological variables. When providing support to an anxious person, it is critical to keep these aspects in mind. Instead of assuming that someone's ostensibly great life events nullify their unpleasant emotions, try affirming the worried sensations they're expressing to you.

Helpful Things to Say to Someone Who is Anxious

The most crucial component of any of these statements is that you must be ready to assist as best you can when the time comes. I try not to get too involved if I am going through a difficult time since I cannot help someone else unless I first heal myself.

Essentially, if you're having a lot of worry yourself, now may not be the best time to give assistance and support. However, if you believe you are in a stable mental state and can continue to be present for a loved one, consult this list of what to and should not say when checking in on someone suffering from anxiety.

Get curious
Most people do not grow up with a diverse mental health vocabulary. After centuries of mental health being largely taboo, it may be exceedingly difficult to find the words to discuss something as complex and confusing as worry. Thus, don't be afraid to ask questions.

Approaching a difficult topic with genuine curiosity is one of the simplest yet most effective ways to begin. Opening the conversation with an honest desire to understand what someone is going through can have a life-changing impact. In this case, both sides benefit: the person struggling feels supported and acknowledged, and the person checking in learns more, allowing them to approach future situations with a deeper level of empathy.

So, what exactly does being curious look like? Begin with an open-ended question and a highly specific assertion. Something like, "I care about you or love you and want to help you as much as I can." Is there anything I can do for you at this time? Then actively listen for and act on the answer.

Another helpful choice is, "Can you describe anything I can do to help you right now? This question is a little more concrete, and concrete questions offer less potential for misunderstandings. This question, like the last one, exhibits unconditional regard, which is important when aiding and talking to someone who is anxious.

Demonstrate care and concern
Phrases like "I love you and I want to help you as best I can" and "I love you and I cannot bear to see you suffering" show your unwavering dedication to your loved one. This provides them with appropriate support that is unrelated to their anxiety or capacity to manage it.

In other words, expressing to your loved one that you have observed a difference in their demeanor and emphasizing that you are here for them is reassuring. You're simply showing the person that their feelings are important. Anxiety can be a distressing and isolating experience, and when a loved one offers assistance, it can create a sense of comfort and allow the individual to feel recognized and nurtured. As a result, they may feel more comfortable opening up and getting help.

Validate their experiences and emotions
While you don't want to talk about yourself, think about sharing your personal anxiety experiences. The important thing is to say something like, 'I've been there' or 'I hear you; it must be so difficult or frustrating,' to show the person that their feeling are normal and that they are not alone. Validation, which involves reflecting a person's emotions back to them and making them feel heard, helps emotion management and rapidly calms the nervous system, which is critical when dealing with anxiety.

You can also use phrases like "It's totally alright to not be okay," "Be kind to yourself," and "It's fine to take pauses," all of which are soothing and put your loved one at rest while not disregarding their suffering and struggle.

Chapter 4

Professional Help

Though there are many different types of anxiety disorders, research suggests that most are caused by similar underlying processes. People with anxiety disorders are often overwhelmed by their emotions, and they react negatively to unpleasant experiences and events.

People frequently try to cope with their negative reactions by avoiding events or experiences that cause them anxiety. Regrettably, avoiding situations can backfire and make anxiety worse.

Psychologists are trained to diagnose anxiety issues and offer patients healthy, more effective coping strategies. Cognitive-behavioral therapy (CBT) is a highly effective type of psychotherapy for treating anxiety disorders. Using CBT, psychologists teach patients how to recognize and manage the variables that contribute to their anxiety.

Patients can better grasp how their ideas affect their anxiety symptoms by utilizing the cognitive component of therapy. They can minimize the frequency and severity of anxiety symptoms by learning to shift their mental habits.

Patients learn strategies to lessen undesirable behaviors linked to anxiety disorders during the behavioral component. Patients are specifically taught to approach activities and situations that cause anxiety, such as public speaking or being in an enclosed space, with the expectation that their feared consequences, such as losing their train of thought or having a panic attack, will be uncommon.

Psychologists and patients engage in a cooperative process known as psychotherapy to pinpoint specific issues and develop useful techniques and strategies for managing anxiety. Patients should anticipate using their new abilities outside of sessions to control anxiety in potentially uncomfortable situations. However, psychologists will not put patients in such situations unless they are confident they have the ability to adequately tackle their concerns.

In addition to cognitive behavioral therapy, psychologists may utilize additional treatments to treat anxiety problems. Group psychotherapy, which often involves multiple people with anxiety disorders, can be useful for both anxiety treatment and patient support.

Family psychotherapy can assist family members in comprehending their loved one's anxiety and learning how to engage in ways that do not reinforce anxious behaviors. Family therapy can be especially beneficial for children and adolescents who suffer from anxiety disorders.

Anxiety problems are highly curable. Most patients with anxiety are able to lessen or eliminate symptoms after a few or fewer months of psychotherapy, and many see relief after just a few visits.

Chapter 5

Self-Care for Supporters

Balancing your own commitments with your caregiver job might make it seem hard to care for yourself. Caregivers frequently feel terrible or selfish about taking time for themselves. Some are concerned that something will happen to their loved ones if they are not present.

If you need to be a caretaker for an extended period of time, you must take care of yourself. This can improve your mood and help you care for your loved one more effectively. Set some weekly goals to take care of yourself. Small, attainable goals prepare you for success. For example, instead of promising to get more sleep, try getting to bed 15 minutes earlier each night. When you fulfill little goals, you feel a surge of energy that motivates you to keep going.

Perform modest physical activities
Engaging in mild exercise can improve your mood and lower your stress levels. Take a walk or a short bike ride outside to enjoy the fresh air and sunshine.

Spend time with your friends and family
Create a support system to stay in touch with people who can help you and chat about your experiences. Anxiety and your caring responsibilities can make this difficult to do. Having a support system might help you reduce stress and feel better.

Prioritise tasks
Being a caregiver has numerous tasks. It may feel as if you need to complete all of these chores at once, but this is not feasible. Decide what you need to do first to keep organized and feel less overwhelmed. You might find it useful to make a checklist of the tasks you need to complete today, this week, or this month. If you don't know how to prioritize tasks, ask for help.

Try relaxing techniques

Relaxation practices can help you deal with your anxiety. Deep breathing, meditation, and applying pressure to specific places of your body can all help you relax.

Check in with yourself

Ask yourself how you're feeling and analyze your own feelings. Some caregivers find it beneficial to keep a journal. Others find it beneficial to jot down their ideas and feelings. Some people prefer to express themselves through art, yoga, and dance.

Ask for assistance and accept it

Ask friends and relatives for assistance with household tasks or meal preparation. Accept help when you are offered it. It is common to feel bad about receiving aid, yet seeking assistance does not indicate weakness or failure. The less stressed you are, the better you will be able to care for your loved one and yourself.

Conclusion

Helping someone with anxiety can take many forms, including educating yourself about the problem, forming a social support network, and obtaining professional help.

Knowing how to help with anxiety can be extremely beneficial to a family member, friend, or even yourself, as everyone experiences worry and fear from time to time. Others, however, suffer from extreme anxiety, which can be difficult to manage.

This highlights the significance of assisting someone suffering from anxiety caused by persons or situations. Showing a person acceptance and support during a difficult moment can help them overcome a hurdle to successfully deal with their condition.

Know what to avoid doing

Know what to avoid, because certain responses that you believe may be beneficial to someone suffering from anxiety may fact be the reverse. For example, promoting fear or anxiety, forcing conflict, or urging the anxious individual to calm down may all have negative consequences.

Enabling anxiety entails going out of your way to help your anxious loved one avoid having to do things yourself. While this may appear thoughtful and innocuous at first, doing things for them and constantly avoiding things to accommodate them may wind up increasing their anxiety and eventually shrinking their environment.

While you should support persons with anxiety to help themselves overcome their concerns, you should equally avoid forcing them to do something they are uncomfortable with. A mental health expert can help them face their concerns progressively and more successfully.

Telling an anxious person to calm down may appear to be an innocent suggestion; nevertheless, encouraging a person suffering from anxiety to just stop feeling what they are feeling is not a good idea. These types of statements can leave people feeling disregarded and misunderstood.

Knowing what not to do while assisting someone with anxiety allows you to provide the appropriate amount of assistance without overdoing it. One challenge to this phase is that an anxious person may not always want to talk about how they feel, so they may not tell you if you're being helpful.

However, it is one of the finest ways to help someone with anxiety since being sensitive to the needs of anxious people allows you to behave in a way that makes them feel better and calmer.

Knowing what to avoid while interacting with someone suffering from anxiety may be more difficult than the other methods listed above, especially if you come from a highly stigmatized culture.

Use efficient anxiety tips
Use appropriate anxiety strategies, such as validation and a network of practical and emotional support. Validating someone's emotional experience indicates that you accept where they are coming from.

On the other side, social support can help to develop a network of practical and emotional assistance. This support network consists of the anxious person's friends and relatives.

Both are essential in assisting a person to manage the effects of anxiety in a variety of aspects of their life. Providing affirmation, as well as practical and emotional support, can help someone with anxiety develop a stable sense of self and good coping mechanisms for dealing with setbacks.

When you disagree with what the anxious person is saying, it might be difficult to validate them. However, it is important to realize that you do not have to agree with someone in order to validate their experience and understand why they feel the way they do.

Despite this, recognizing someone's feelings and providing emotional support are still some of the finest methods to aid someone suffering from anxiety because these simple gestures may be a huge encouragement to anyone experiencing them.

Using such excellent anxiety tips may be more challenging to put into practice because they should stem from an attempt to connect on a very deep level and should be a natural part of how you engage with someone who is anxious.

Express concern
Express concern by asking how you may assist a loved one who is suffering from anxiety. It's never easy to observe someone experiencing an anxiety attack or other signs that they're suffering from anxiety.
Ask your loved one what you can do to assist them deal with situations that cause them anxiety, as well as how you can offer support during those difficult times. This might reassure your loved one that someone will be present to provide them with a safe area in which to let their fear lessen.

Having someone who comes from a position of concern can help an individual suffering from anxiety by letting them know that there is someone who can offer support and listen without judgment.

The desire to give counsel, which some people may find emotionally invalidating, is one possible impediment to showing real concern for others. After all, most people suffering from anxiety simply want someone to listen to their concerns and may not want advice from those outside of the scenario. Expressing worry, on the other hand, is one of the most effective methods to assist a loved one with an anxiety illness since it improves their well-being and offers them a stronger feeling of social connection.

Compared to other methods of assisting someone with anxiety, expressing or demonstrating your care for a loved one may be easier because you understand how to approach them from a place of love, worry, and respect.

Avoid pressing them
Avoid forcing an anxious friend or family member to accomplish something they are very concerned about. While we have discussed the significance of avoiding enabling their behaviors, we must also avoid forcing them to do anything they are uncomfortable with.

This step is crucial because it shows your loved one that you value their time and enable them to proceed at their own speed.

Not putting pressure on someone with anxiety also helps to boost their self-confidence and belief in themselves because they realize they don't have to rush into something to feel good or accepted.

When you get into perfectionist behaviors, you may find it difficult to put pressure on someone suffering from anxiety. Many perfectionists fail to recognize that there are better ways to do things without beating themselves up, and they may transfer these tendencies onto others.

Avoiding pressure on a loved one suffering from anxiety is one of the most effective strategies to help them cope with the disease since it instills in them a strong sense of confidence, which can help them think positively, thus creating a healthier mental state.

Keeping yourself from placing pressure on someone suffering from anxiety, especially if they are a friend or family member, should be simple once you realize that any form of pressure will only exacerbate their worry.

Ask how you can help
Ask how you can assist and convey your readiness to support them in difficult circumstances. Determine what you can do to help them feel better when they are confronted with situations that make them anxious. You may be startled to learn that your loved one has already prepared an answer.

Finding out how you can help is vital because it eliminates guesswork and demonstrates that you care about them. This phase can also assist someone with anxiety to describe how they want to be supported, allowing them to be more open about their feelings.

It is important to note, however, that some people find it difficult to disclose themselves. This can create a barrier that prevents you from assisting a loved one who is anxious.

Knowing how to assist a friend or family member suffering from anxiety is one of the most effective methods to alleviate their burden because having someone to turn to can help them manage daily obstacles, particularly during a crisis.

This stage may also be simple for most people because people in general desire to assist more than we give them credit for, and performing acts of kindness typically makes them feel better.

Encourage them to get help
Encourage them to seek help, which can take many forms, including talking to loved ones, joining a support group, or getting psychological treatment.

This phase is crucial because adequate social support can aid in the development of resilience to anxiety and the regulation of its consequences. Encouraging your loved one to seek assistance can also benefit them in another way, as having a personal support system can give them a sense of belonging, which develops a sense of security and, eventually, leads to better mental health.

The unwillingness of a loved one to seek treatment can be a barrier to pushing them to do so. Some people may be hesitant to reach out to others because they are uncomfortable speaking in front of a group, whilst others may battle with pride and distrust.

However, encouraging someone to get treatment is one of the most effective strategies to help them overcome their anxiety since it creates a sense of security, which facilitates the expression of mental and emotional needs.

Finally, urging a person to get therapy may be more difficult than other ways to assist someone with anxiety since, at the end of the day, it is a personal decision that the patient must make, and pushing the concept may cause additional problems in your relationship.

Encourage them to consult with a therapist
Encourage them to see a therapist if you observe that their anxiety is interfering with their daily activities. You can accomplish this by volunteering to accompany them to a therapy appointment or supporting them in compiling a list of their worries.

This stage in assisting someone with anxiety is critical because obtaining help from a mental health expert allows your loved one to identify the underlying issues that may be contributing to their illness. Another benefit of therapy for someone suffering from anxiety is the formation of healthy habits to regain control of uncomfortable situations, which is a skill taught with the assistance of a certified professional.

Dread of judgment, a conviction that their ailment isn't serious, dread of what they could learn in therapy, or fear of diagnosis are some of the reasons why people are hesitant to see a therapist.

Despite these possible difficulties, seeing a therapist is one of the most effective ways to help someone with anxiety since a qualified mental health professional can assist them in better understanding their own emotions.

Convincing someone you care about to go to therapy may be more challenging than the other methods given in this chapter for assisting a person with anxiety because it needs careful planning to say the right thing and choose the perfect time to urge a loved one.

Offer to help them schedule a medical visit

Offer to help them schedule a medical visit with an anxiety therapist. Seeking therapy services for a loved one may also include providing relevant information to the scheduler, such as your loved one's name, age, and residence, as well as the symptoms he or she is experiencing.

This stage is critical because it can pave the way for your loved one's full recovery. It's also worth mentioning that you don't have to force them to commit to long-term treatment; instead, encourage them to attend a few sessions and ask what they think.

Supporting someone's effort to book an appointment with a therapist can assist the patient feel as if they can draw strength from a friend during difficult times in their lives.

If a loved one has a negative attitude toward mental health treatment in general, it may be difficult to assist them in scheduling their first therapy session. If they do, they may not believe that treatment may solve their problem.

Still, offering to assist them with booking an appointment with a therapist is one of the most effective methods to help them overcome anxiety since merely being present can have a beneficial impact on how they approach therapy.

Finally, volunteering to help a loved one schedule their therapy session may be easier than the other anxiety-relieving activities described in this piece, as long as the patient has decided to seek professional care.

Tailor your support to their preferences and connection style

Adjust your support based on your loved one's preferences and attachment style. After all, it is advisable to personalize your assistance to their psychological and emotional requirements. In this manner, you allow children to set boundaries while prioritizing their comfort. Attachment styles investigate the relationships between a kid and his or her caregiver and how they influence the child's subsequent development and attachment patterns.

For example, those with an avoidant attachment style, who have previously experienced rejection in caregiving or relationships, respond best to strong displays of actual practical support. Others, on the other hand, are more likely to demand emotional support owing to a fear of desertion or of their feelings being too overwhelming for others, particularly those who are deeply bonded or have a "preoccupied" attachment style.

Understanding a person's anxiety preferences and attachment style is critical since it improves treatment experiences and outcomes. This stage is very advantageous for the patient since it demonstrates that you value their self-awareness and fosters trust in the relationship.

A potential stumbling block at this level is a lack of understanding of people's attachment styles. This leads to a misunderstanding of a person's strengths and shortcomings in a relationship. Listening to your loved one's preferences is one of the most effective forms of anxiety attack support you can provide because involving them in decision-making during their rehabilitation can enhance engagement and attempts to reach long-term objectives.

This phase, however, may be more difficult than others because it demands an understanding of a person's attachment types and how to respond to their needs based on their attachment patterns.

Stop treating the person you love as a machine
Stop treating your loved one like a machine and recognize that he or she is a human being capable of experiencing complicated emotions. Do not dismiss their sentiments as something they can simply get over or rationalize away.

Treating your loved one's struggle as if it were incorrect or inappropriate is a harmful form of emotional abuse that can impair their ability to control their own emotions.

Someone who is anxious can benefit from avoiding this since it will prevent them from feeling as though their subjective emotional experience is unimportant. Rather than approaching children as if they are inanimate objects, it is possible to teach them that their emotions are valuable and that they need not fear criticism.

One potential issue with this phase is being unable to absorb another person's feelings or not knowing how to respond to them since they may be concerned with their own personal problems.

However, it is critical to avoid invalidating emotions, as it is one of the most effective strategies to treat anxiety because it helps people identify their feelings and affirm their sense of identity.

This step, however, may be easier said than done because humans are built toward negativity. This means that we react more strongly to negative stimuli, making it more difficult for certain people to focus on the positive and accept others' bad feelings.

Offer soothing physical contact.
Make soothing physical contact with your loved one. This can aid in reducing his or her emotional anguish. Providing reassuring physical contact can consequently have a good psychological and physiological impact. Furthermore, for someone who suffers from anxiety, social touch can be relaxing and help to lessen feelings of worry.

One potential impediment to completing this stage is if the individual who is expected to provide comfort is uncomfortable making physical touch with others, or vice versa. However, some people find it difficult to engage in reassuring physical contact because limits must first be set, as well as knowing how comfortable you and your loved one are with physical touch.

Find ways to support and care for your loved one.
Look for ways to support and care for your loved one, such as providing anxiety-related ideas and resources, discovering items that

can help them relax, and introducing them to relaxation practices like as deep breathing and meditation.

Knowing what else they can do to reduce their anxiety can be beneficial. For example, avoiding alcohol and drugs, reducing caffeine intake, increasing physical exercise, and practicing relaxation techniques such as deep breathing and meditation have all been demonstrated to reduce anxiety.

These additional techniques to support and care for your loved one can be beneficial because they can be used as non-medication anxiety treatments. However, because this stage involves someone who is prepared to put forth the effort to find ways to properly support and care for a loved one suffering from anxiety, a potential impediment is a lack of understanding of mental health as a public health issue.

This can be problematic because if someone holds incorrect views or perceptions about mental health concerns, they may be unwilling to provide a helping hand at all.

Going out of your way to support someone suffering from anxiety is one of the most effective methods to help them deal. Having someone you can trust and rely on during difficult times may be really motivating.

Providing a supporting relationship to a loved one is easier than the other methods described here for how to help anxiety, as long as you have the willingness and compassion to do it.

Tell your loved ones that they deserve to be healthy
Tell your loved one that they deserve to be healthy, and keep reminding them that mental health is equally vital as physical health. According to the CDC's About Mental Health page, depression increases the risk of a variety of physical problems, including diabetes and stroke.

Similarly, chronic diseases can increase the risk of mental health issues. Thus, it is critical to remind our loved ones that their physical and mental health are both significant components of our overall well-being.

Another advantage of this reminder for a loved one suffering from anxiety is that they will be reminded that they deserve better and are worth it. Telling someone that they deserve to be healthy may be difficult if you already have too much on your plate and are unable to take on additional obligations.

Being present for your loved one to continually remind them to stay healthy or take their prescriptions is one of the most effective methods to help them manage anxiety since it takes their focus away from what causes their worry.

Some people may find it easier to remind a friend or family member to keep healthy by just checking in with them on a frequent basis, asking how they are, and staying in touch.

Assist your loved one with future planning
Assist your loved one with future planning, remembering that their mental and emotional demands may alter in the future. If, for example, you are no longer able to care for your loved one due to unexpected circumstances, you might create a list of activities you do for him or her to help with the transition of assistance.

Being active in your loved one's future planning is vital since, as the person who provided support, you know enough about them and how they manage their illness on a daily basis.

This might also benefit your loved one by encouraging them to see a brighter future for themselves. It also makes children excited about new activities and individuals they will meet in the future.

Other new responsibilities, such as beginning your own family, and a deteriorating relationship with your loved one are two potential barriers to your involvement in future planning for them.

Still, assisting with future care planning is one of the best ways for a
loved one with acute anxiety to cope with their situation since it
allows them to set long-term goals, which can boost their drive to
stick to their treatment plan.